The Illustrated Imprints
of Isaiah Thomas

The Illustrated Imprints
of Isaiah Thomas

Barbara E. Lacey

American Philosophical Society Press
Philadelphia • 2014

Transactions of the
American Philosophical Society
Held at Philadelphia
For Promoting Useful Knowledge
Volume 104, Part 2

ISBN: 978-1-60618-042-6

US ISSN: 0065-9746

Library of Congress Cataloging-in-Publication Data
Lacey, Barbara E., 1937-
    The illustrated imprints of Isaiah Thomas / Barbara E. Lacey.
        pages cm. — (Transactions of the American Philosophical Society held at Philadelphia
for promoting useful knowledge, ISSN 0065-9746 ; volume 104, part 2)
    Includes bibliographical references and index.
    ISBN 978-1-60618-042-6
    1. Thomas, Isaiah, 1749-1831. 2. Illustrated books—Massachusetts—History—18th century—
Bibliography. 3. Printing—Massachusetts—History—18th century. 4. Massachusetts—Imprints.
I. Title.
    Z232.T4L33 2014
    096'.10974409033—dc23
                        2014039653

Contents

Preface

This representative sampling of the illustrated publications of the Massachusetts printer Isaiah Thomas suggests the great variety of eighteenth-century American imprints that used images to enhance or modify the meaning of the text. Chapters dealing with almanacs, children's books, geographies, novels and poetry, magazines, and the Bible show how word and image sometimes work together, occasionally contradict each other, and almost always provide a more nuanced, composite view of the subject.

The frontispiece of William Hill Brown's sentimental novel *The Power of Sympathy*, published by Thomas in 1789, for example, is not simply an eye-catching decoration. Portraying the heroine taking poison, it asks the reader to consider whether the moral implications that this image suggests are born out in the text of the novel.

This brief volume attempts to bridge the gaps among several scholarly fields, including art history, literary criticism, the study of visual culture, and the history of the book. Illustrations are treated here as material artifacts and not judged exclusively on their artistic merit, and are analyzed for what they say about early American values, ideas, attitudes, and assumptions.

This volume will be of interest to students of early American history and art, to American Studies scholars, and to general readers curious about early book publication and illustration.

Acknowledgments

I am indebted to many people and institutions for the opportunity to study illustrated imprints in early America. The librarians, collections, and policies of the American Antiquarian Society (AAS), Worcester, Massachusetts, and the Homer Babbidge Library at the University of Connecticut, Storrs, Connecticut, provided the environment for preliminary research. A National Endowment for the Humanities Fellowship enabled me to explore archives at the AAS, which hold the originals of the imprints reproduced in this study. At an AAS seminar, I presented a paper on Isaiah Thomas, printer and publisher, which was related to a more extensive work subsequently published: *From Sacred to Secular: Visual Images in Early American Publications* (University of Delaware Press, 2007). The Isaiah Thomas seminar paper was further developed and substantially expanded for the American Philosophical Society. I am deeply grateful to Mary McDonald, Editor and Director of Publications, and to the Committee on Publications at the American Philosophical Society, for keen interest, helpful advice, and useful suggestions.

I was fortunate to have computer assistance at critical moments from my daughter, Elizabeth Laliberte; and Jim Lacey, my husband and friend, has always provided suggestions, support, and editorial advice in the course of my work. The faculty and staff of the University of Saint Joseph, West Hartford, Connecticut, were helpful in granting sabbatical leave and faculty development funds necessary for my research.

The primary source materials for Isaiah Thomas's imprints, and for my other articles on the subject of eighteenth-century printed illustrations, are those listed by Charles Evans (1850–1933), a bibliographer whose ambition was to record every item printed during the first two hundred years of printing in America. The results of his research were published in the fourteen-volume work, *American Bibliography* (1903–59), and in James E. Moody's compressed *Short-Title Evans* (1969). The electronic format I used to view publications with illustrations was the microcard series, *Early American Imprints,* based on the Evans listing and produced by the Readex Microprint Corporation. A series in microfiche subsequently became available that allowed photocopies of the imprints to be made. More recently, a CD-ROM catalog of the microform series was published and is available at many universities and libraries. Technological changes such as these have democratized historical research, as students and scholars increasingly are able to engage in studies based on original sources, an activity once available only to those who could spend extensive time in far-flung archives where such documents are stored.

Illustrations

Figure 1.1   Frontispiece, by I. Thomas. Erra Pater. *The New Book of Knowledge* (Boston: Z. Fowle [1767]). Courtesy of the American Antiquarian Society.

Figure 1.2   *Mother and Children*, by J. Turner. *History of the Holy Jesus* (Boston: B. Gray, 174?). Courtesy of the Phillips Library, Peabody Essex Museum, Salem, Mass.

Figure 1.3   *Mother and Children*, by I. Thomas. *History of the Holy Jesus* (Boston: Z. Fowle, 1764). Courtesy, American Antiquarian Society.

Figure 1.4   *The Prodigal Daughter,* by I. Thomas (Boston, 1767), 12. Courtesy, American Antiquarian Society.

Figure 1.5   Title page, by P. Fleet. *The Prodigal Daughter* (Boston: [Thomas Fleet, 175?]). Courtesy, American Antiquarian Society.

Figure 3.1   Title page, by P. Revere. Ezra Gleason, *The Massachusetts Calendar for 1774* (Boston: I. Thomas). Courtesy, American Antiquarian Society.

Figure 4.1   *Noah's Ark. A Curious Hierogylyphic Bible* (Worcester, MA: I. Thomas, 1788), 19. Courtesy, American Antiquarian Society.

Figure 4.2   [Mary Jane Kilner]. *The Adventures of a Pincushion: Designed Chiefly for the Use of Young Ladies* (Worcester, MA: I. Thomas, 1788), 11. Courtesy, American Antiquarian Society.

Figure 4.3 *Mother Goose's Melody* (Worcester, MA: I. Thomas, 1794), 64–65. Courtesy, American Antiquarian Society.

Figure 5.1 *Eastern and Western Hemisphere, Map of the World*, by A. Doolittle. Jedidiah Morse, *The American Universal Geography* (Boston: Thomas and Andrews, 1793), 2 vols. Courtesy, American Antiquarian Society.

Figure 6.1 Frontispiece, *The Story of Orphelia*, by S. Hill. *The Power of Sympathy* (Boston: I. Thomas, 1789). Courtesy, American Antiquarian Society.

Figure 6.2 Frontispiece, by J. Seymour. Charlotte Smith, *Elegiac Sonnets* (Worcester, MA: I. Thomas, 1795). Courtesy, American Antiquarian Society.

Figure 7.1 Frontispiece, *Prospect . . . Near the Common*, by S. Hill. *Massachusetts Magazine* (Nov. 1790). Courtesy, American Antiquarian Society.

Figure 7.2 Frontispiece, *View of the State House, Boston*, by S. Hill. *Massachusetts Magazine* (July 1793). Courtesy, American Antiquarian Society.

Figure 8.1 *The Falling of the Walls of Jericho*, by J. Seymour. *The Holy Bible* (Worcester, MA: I. Thomas, 1791), Vol. I. Courtesy, American Antiquarian Society.

Figure 8.2 *Susanna*, by J. Seymour. *The Holy Bible* (Worcester, MA: I. Thomas, 1791), Vol. II. Courtesy, American Antiquarian Society.

Figure 8.3 *Crucifixion*, by J. Seymour, *The Holy Bible* (Worcester, MA: I. Thomas, 1791), Vol. II. Courtesy, American Antiquarian Society.

Figure 8.4 *Michael and the Devil*, by J. Seymour, *The Holy Bible* (Worcester, MA: I. Thomas, 1791), Vol. II. Courtesy, American Antiquarian Society.

Introduction

Isaiah Thomas (1749–1831) became a leading patriot, printer, publisher, and bookseller in the rags-to-riches tradition of the more famous Benjamin Franklin. When he retired in 1802, Thomas was one of the wealthiest men in America. Founder of the American Antiquarian Society in Worcester, Massachusetts, he donated his library and newspaper files to the Society's archive, which became the leading repository of early American imprints.[1] His illustrated productions include cuts, carved with bold, heavy lines into wood or type metal, and engravings, made from a fine network of lines incised on copperplates. The images in these illustrations have an affinity with their texts, and may support, develop, or even change the verbal meaning. Placed in their historical context and analyzed, the illustrated imprints give insight into popular taste and commercial aspects of printing in eighteenth-century America. They also provide evidence of incremental change and persistent practices in artistic production and visual culture, challenging the idea that a new departure took place about this time. Instead of a fundamental shift from a verbal to a more modern visual worldview, which would imply a sharp break from plain texts to illustrated material, the imprints of Isaiah Thomas reveal a continuum of blended image and text. If there were changes, they were gradual, not seismic.

Although some historians have been reluctant to pay close attention to images in their research, new fields, such as the history of the book,

---

[1] On the past and present goals of the American Antiquarian Society, see Marcus A. McCorison, "Isaiah Thomas, the American Antiquarian Society, and the Future," *Proceedings of the American Antiquarian Society* 91, no. I (1981): 27–37.

and scholars of "word and image" studies have addressed the subject of illustrations directly in their conferences, research, and publications. W. J. T. Mitchell suggests that recent literary criticism has taken a "pictorial turn, a paradigm shift involving encounters with and concerns about the visual,"[2] whereas other critics have provided a visual grammar of compositional structures and keys to the conventions of visual semiotics.[3] By analyzing the image as well as the accompanying text, critics point to new complexities of meaning. This study calls attention to a paradox: Thomas's imprints drew on European literary and artistic traditions at the same time as he hoped to gain international status for a distinctly American product. This dual tendency will be found in the examination of the productions of Isaiah Thomas in three areas: his own early rudimentary woodcuts; his later employment of American engravers for children's books, fiction, and periodicals; and, ultimately, Thomas's *Holy Bible* of 1791, a cultural landmark of technical production and visual content that marks him as a dedicated patron of the arts.

---

[2] W. J. T. Mitchell, *Picture Theory: Essays in Verbal and Visual Representation* (Chicago: University of Chicago Press, 1994), 1–34.

[3] Gunther Kress and Theo van Leeuwen, *Reading Images: The Grammar of Visual Design* (London: Routledge, 1996); George H. Roeder, Jr., "Filling In the Picture: Visual Culture," *Reviews in American History* 26 (March 1998): 275–93.

1

Rudimentary Woodcuts

Born into a poor family, at age six Isaiah Thomas was indentured as an apprentice to Zechariah Fowle, a Boston printer and seller of ballads and peddler's books.[1] He records setting up a ballad, *The Lawyer's Pedigree*, before he could read. Thomas would boast that when he was about ten years old, he "had the whole management of Fowle's printing office, that is, he did the work in his own way, & corrected the Press, as well as he could, and when a form was ready, Fowle having no other help assisted at Press."[2] In addition to learning the rudiments of printing, Thomas experimented with the craft of cutting wood or type metal to create illustrations for small books. As he notes in his autobiography,

> At this time there was scarcely a person in Boston, who could cut on wood or type metal; this induced I. T. to attempt the business to decorate the ballads and pedlars pamphlets issued from Fowle's Press; He executed above an 100 of them and sorry enough, but they answered the purpose, and were nearly a match for those executed by a negro of old Thomas Fleet. Fleet, altho' he printed a newspaper was also a Printer of ballads, &. In this business of ballad printing Fowle was his rival.[3]

At an early stage of his life, Thomas demonstrated his budding interest in the visual. The illustrations for three publications are attributed to him: *The Book of Knowledge* (1762), *The History of the Holy Jesus* (1764), and *The Prodigal Daughter* (1768). A note in his handwriting in the 1767 Boston edition of *The Book of Knowledge* (a simplified encyclopedia), states that he printed and made the cuts for the original edition of this work for Z. Fowle, in 1762, as an apprentice when he was age 13.[4] The cuts for *The Book of Knowledge* include a varied offering: the frontispiece, the man of signs, a diagram related to bloodletting, a depiction

---

[1] Richard F. Hixson, "Isaiah Thomas," in *American National Biography*, eds. John Garraty and Mark Carnes (New York: Oxford University Press, 1999), 21:508–10; Richard C. Steele, *Isaiah Thomas* (Worcester, MA: Worcester Telegram and Gazette, Inc. and Worcester Historical Museum, 1981); Clifford K. Shipton, *Isaiah Thomas: Printer, Patriot and Philanthropist, 1749–1831* (Rochester, NY: Leo Hart, 1948); Charles Lemuel Nichols, *Isaiah Thomas: Printer, Writer and Collector* (1912; repr. New York: Burt Franklin, 1967).

[2] Isaiah Thomas, Isaiah Thomas Papers, Box 1, Folder 2 undated, American Antiquarian Society, Worcester, MA, MS Autobiography, ii.

[3] Isaiah Thomas Papers, Box I. Folder 2 undated, American Antiquarian Society, Worcester, MA. MS Autobiography, ii; see also Isaiah Thomas, *Three Autobiographical Fragments* (Worcester, MA: American Antiquarian Society, 1962).

[4] Card catalog entry for *The Book of Knowledge*, American Antiquarian Society. An important guide to early American wood and metal cuts is Elizabeth Carroll Reilly, *A Dictionary of Colonial American Printers' Ornaments and Illustrations* (Worcester, MA: American Antiquarian Society, 1975).

and explanation of "Moles in Man or Woman," "a Wheel of Fortune," and a "portable instrument to find the Hour of the Day."

The frontispiece to *The Book of Knowledge*, reprinted in several almanacs, is the most interesting illustration (Figure 1.1). It shows a man standing in the midst of scientific instruments, including calipers, quadrant, and a globe, while viewed through a cross-staff. This ancient instrument, recorded as first used in the fourteenth century, measured the elevation of a star, relative to the horizon, in order to calculate latitude.[5] Although commonly used to calculate a ship's position, the figure in the frontispiece is not shown at sea; instead, he is located in a carefully drawn scene that includes a starry sky, two buildings, several hills, and a tree. The presence of the cross-staff in an illustration as late as the eighteenth century might be explained by its low cost, which kept it in the hands of navigators long after more accurate instruments for use at sea had been developed, or more likely, the illustration is a copy of an older cut.

The History of the Holy Jesus, reprinted dozens of time over the course of the century, was issued by Zechariah Fowle in Boston about 1764.[6] The initials "I. T." appear on eight of the cuts.[7] Certain of the cuts appear to have been re-engraved from those that James Turner made for editions printed in the 1740s. The cuts by Thomas are the reverse of the earlier cuts, though he introduced some changes, such as a window in his version of "The careful Mother instructing her Children" (Figures 1.2 and 1. 3). Although they are "very crude and not the equal of the originals," they were used again in the 1774 edition.[8]

The illustrations in *The History of the Holy Jesus* provide tantalizing glimpses into the prescribed role of women in mideighteenth-century American society. The illustration of a mother and her children shows a full-length figure seated in a curved-back chair, holding up for viewing

---

[5]M. V. Brewington, "Notes on the Cross-Staff," *American Neptune* 14 (1954): 187–91; I thank Britta Karlberg, Peaboxdy Essex Museum Library, Salem, Massachusetts, for this reference. The cut also appears in *Thomas's New England Almanac for 1775* and was recut for *Bickerstaff's Almanac for 1786.* Marion Barber Stowell describes the instrument as a "Jacob staff"; *Early American Almanacs: The Colonial Weekday Bible* (New York: Burt Franklin, 1977), 96, 90.

[6]Albert Carlos Bates, *The History of the Holy Jesus: A List of Editions of this Once Popular Children's Book* (Hartford: n.p., 1911).

[7]Sinclair Hamilton, *Early American Book Illustrators and Wood Engravers, 1670–1870,* 2 vols. (Princeton: Princeton University Press, 1958) I, xxix; Reilly, *Ornaments and Illustrations,* 303.

[8]Hamilton, I, xxix, 22–23. A word of caution about these attributes is given by Martha Gandy Fales, "James Turner, Silversmith-Engraver," in *Prints of New England,* ed. Georgia Brady Barnhill (Worcester, MA: American Antiquarian Society, 1991), 4.

Frontifpiece *to the* Book *of* Knowledge

Figure 1.1 Frontispiece, by I. Thomas. Erra Pater. *The New Book of Knowledge* (Boston: Z. Fowle [1767]).
Courtesy of the American Antiquarian Society.

Figure 1.2 *Mother and Children*, by J. Turner. *History of the Holy Jesus* (Boston: B. Gray, 174?).
Courtesy of the Phillips Library, Peabody Essex Museum, Salem, Mass.

a page representing a book, perhaps a Bible.[9] On the right are two young women, half-length figures in laced bodices, representing her daughters. Before her is a swaddled child in a cradle, while behind her is a young boy in a frock coat. All five figures look with full face at the viewer, who seems to have surprised them as they engage in an intimate domestic scene. The scene involves religious instruction for the young, who range in age from infant to young adult and includes both sexes. The image suggests the responsibility for such instruction lies with the mother.[10]

---

[9] A double column of print in an illustration of a book was often used by an engraver to represent a Bible, as in the Turner illustration; Hugh Amory, *Bibliography and the Book Trades: Studies in the Print Culture of Early New England* (Philadelphia: University of Pennsylvania Press, 2005), 27. Thomas, in contrast, uses simple crosshatching in his illustration of a book.

[10] On women's literacy, see E. Jennifer Moneghan, *Learning to Read and Write in Colonial America* (Amherst: University of Massachusetts Press, 2005). The implications of literacy are considered by David D. Hall, "The Uses of Literacy in New England, 1600–1850," in *Printing and Society in Early America*, eds. William L. Joyce, David D. Hall, Richard D. Brown, and John B. Hench (Worcester, MA: American Antiquarian Society, 1983), 1–47.

The careful *Mother* Inftructing her Children.

Figure 1.3 *Mother and Children*, by I. Thomas. *History of the Holy Jesus* (Boston: Z. Fowle, 1764).
Courtesy, American Antiquarian Society.

A third set of cuts by the young Isaiah was made for the chapbook, *The Prodigal Daughter.*[11] The title is related thematically to the New Testament parable of the Prodigal Son (Luke 15:11–32), a popular theme in Christian art since the thirteenth century. The image on the title page of *The Prodigal Daughter,* found also in the interior of the work, does not refer to a particular moment in the story, but rather, like medieval narrative illustration, is a multiple of individual episodes, each embodied in a single figure (Figure 1. 4). To the left is the silhouetted figure of a woman who holds a handkerchief up to her face; she is the mother who

---

[11] On popular print in early New England, see David D. Hall, *Worlds of Wonder, Days of Judgment: Popular Religious Belief in Early New England* (New York: Alfred A. Knopf, 1989). The Fowle imprint of *The Prodigal Daughter* is listed by Evans as printed in 1767, the last year in which Thomas worked as Fowle's apprentice, but the cuts may have been made earlier and the book printed between 1763 and 1771. In 1770, after a brief partnership with Fowle, Thomas purchased his press and printing materials and came into possession of many old cuts, along with some he made for his master, and included them in a later edition of *The Prodigal Daughter.*

(12)

She in her Coffin then was carried home,
And when unto her Father's Houfe fhe come,
She in her Coffin fat, and did admire
Her winding Sheet, and thus fhe did defire,
　The worthy Minifter for to fit down,
And fhe would tell him Wonders which were fhown
Unto her, fince her Soul had took it's Flight,
She had feen the Regions of eternal Night.

　　　　　　　　　　　　　　　　　She

Figure 1.4 *The Prodigal Daughter*, by I. Thomas (Boston, 1767), 12.
Courtesy, American Antiquarian Society.

The Prodigal Daughter:

Or a ſtrange and wonderful Relation, ſhewing, how a Gentleman of a vaſt Eſtate in *Briſtol*, had a proud and diſobedient Daughter, who becauſe her Parents would not ſupport her in all her Extravagance, bargained with the Devil to poiſon them. How an Angel informed her Parents of their Daughter's Deſign. How ſhe lay in a Trance four Days, and when ſhe was put into the Grave, ſhe came to Life again, and related the wonderful Things ſhe ſaw in the other World. Likewiſe the Subſtance of a Sermon preached on this Occaſion by the Reverend Mr *Williams*, from *Luke* 15. 24.

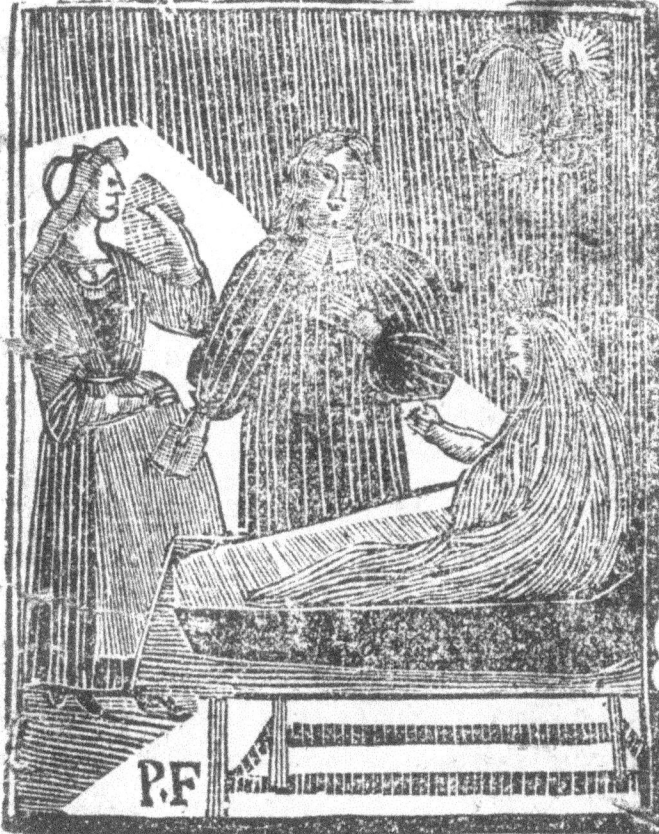

Printed and ſold at the Heart and Crown in Cornhill, *Boſton*.

Figure 1.5   Title page, by P. Fleet. *The Prodigal Daughter* (Boston: [Thomas Fleet, 175?]). Courtesy, American Antiquarian Society.

wipes away tears shed over a wayward child. The central mediating figure is the minister, shown full face, one hand over the heart, the other holding a book; he represents the word of God transforming religious experience important to the climax of the plot. To the right, in profile, is the daughter who melodramatically sits up in her shroud and coffin, with hands extended to receive communion, representing the happy conclusion. The scene is dark, but a fixture with a candle above the daughter provides sufficient illumination for the penitential scene.

The Thomas frontispiece for *The Prodigal Daughter* may be compared to the one by "P. F.," or Pompey Fleet, Thomas Fleet's black slave who worked the Fleet press and carved all of its chapbook cuts (Figure 1.5). The cut by P. F. seems more decisive and skillful, but the Thomas cut shows an improved sense of two-dimensional design. One cutter may have copied the other, but the original was probably a chapbook imported from London or Dublin. Thomas later wrote about this competitor:

> [He] was an ingenious man, and cut, on wooden blocks, all the pictures which decorate the ballads and small books of his master. Fleet had also two negro boys born in his house; sons, I believe, to the man just mentioned, whom he brought up to work at press and case; one named Pompey and the other Cesar; they were young when their master died; but they remained in the family, and continued to labor regularly in the printing house with the sons of Mr. Fleet, who succeeded their father, until the constitution of Massachusetts, adopted in 1780, made them freemen.[12]

In these early works, Thomas shows his familiarity with some of the staples of popular religion, including medieval tales, biblical abridgements, and ancient folklore. Though immature as art work, his cuts give clear and vivid evidence of familiar themes one could expect when turning to these illustrated almanacs and chapbooks.

---

[12] Isaiah Thomas, *The History of Printing in America*, 2 vols. (Albany, NY: 1874; repr. New York: Burt Franklin, 1971), 1:99.

2

Establishing a Printing Business

Thomas next made his mark by publishing newspapers, an important genre that, by midcentury, comprised eighty percent of all American publications.[1] He first worked briefly *at The Halifax Gazette* and *The New Hampshire Gazette*, then later published *The Massachusetts Spy*, and eventually, emboldened by success, started *The Royal American Magazine*.[2] In a recollection stated with some irony, he describes Daniel Fowle's creation of a masthead for *The New Hampshire Gazette*:

> Fowle had several type metal cuts, which had been engraved and used for an abridgement of Croxall's Esop; and as he thought that there should be something ornamental in the title of the Gazette, and not finding an artist to engrave anything appropriate, he introduced one of these cuts, designed for the fable of the crow and the fox. This cut was, in a short time, broken by some accident, and he supplied its place by one engraved for the fable of Jupiter and the peacock. This was used until worn down, when another cut from the fables was substituted. Eventually, the royal arms, badly engraved, appeared, and at the same time, "Historical Chronicle" was added to the title; a cut of the king's arms well executed, afterwards took the place of the other.[3]

Thomas gives an accurate example of the degeneration of woodcuts and metal cuts in the course of the eighteenth century. Type cuts, fonts, and presses passed from one printer to another, and the same illustration was used for completely different subjects. Old cuts were worn from constant use, and new illustrations were frequently crude replications.[4] Yet, the implication of his remark is that at an early age he knew the difference between superior cuts and makeshift practices.

By spring of 1767, Thomas was back at Fowle's shop in Boston with the rank of journeyman, staying long enough to be released from his apprenticeship and to make plans for travel to England in order to improve his printing skills. The trip to England never materialized, and following two years in the Carolinas, Thomas once more returned to Boston. After buying out Fowle, he began publishing *The Massachusetts Spy*, which

---

[1] Charles E. Clark, "Early American Journalism: News and Opinion in the Popular Press," in *A History of the Book in America Vol. One: The Colonial Book in the Atlantic World*, eds. Hugh Amory and David D. Hall (Cambridge: Cambridge University Press, 2000), 355.

[2] Isaiah Thomas, *The History of Printing in America*, 2 vols. (Albany, NY: 1874; repr. New York: Burt Franklin, 1971), 11:61, 64–65, 77–79.

[3] Ibid., 335.

[4] Harry B. Weiss, *A Book About Chapbooks: The People's Literature of Bygone Times* (1942; repr. Hatboro, PA: Folklore Associates, 1969), 4–5.

soon vigorously denounced British rule. After British occupation of the city, for safety he moved his presses to Worcester, where he published *The Worcester Spy* for nearly a quarter of a century. For visual interest, it used small cuts to advertise the sale of farms and houses, and in the 1790s, the paper was emblazoned with an unusual masthead; two putti carry Thomas's name on a banner up to the heavens. Although new in Worcester, and probably misunderstood by Thomas, the motif had been used since Roman times on sarcophagi to praise the illustrious dead.

3

Newspapers and Almanacs

Once relocated in Worcester, Thomas began expanding his printing business, despite his observation that "Arts and Arms are not very agreeable Companions."[1] Encouraged by the success of *The Spy*, in 1774 he began to publish *The Royal American Magazine*, a monthly with engravings, scholarly articles, and essays. He subscribed to the major British magazines and reviews from which he intended to draw material, and planned to combine this with original work. Steeped in imagery of America's "Rising Glory," it featured some twenty engravings by Paul Revere and Joseph Callender, as well as music, liberty songs, brief fiction, and verse by Phillis Wheatley.[2] Other striking engravings in *The Royal American Magazine*, in addition to Revere's political cartoons, are his portraits of John Hancock and John Adams, and a "View of the Town of Boston, with Ships of War in the Harbour."[3]

Also in 1774, Thomas commissioned a satiric engraving by Revere for the title page of *The Massachusetts Calendar; or An Almanack* (Figure 3.1). It shows Thomas Hutchinson, governor of Massachusetts, seated at a table covered with books, a copy of Machiavelli at his feet. The colonists were familiar with medieval symbolism from its use in political cartoons found in imported English magazines. Here, Revere employs such symbolism in the figure painted like a skeleton who strides toward Hutchinson with a spear, while a grinning devil with horns and sharp teeth holds up the traitor's lengthy "List of Crimes." Hutchinson, represented as "the wicked statesman" about to take leave of the world and receive proper punishment, was unpopular with many colonists for his stand on the Stamp Act and for enforcing the Tea Act. The dramatic woodcut and accompanying text were meant to politicize readers and intimidate Loyalists into support for revolt against the British. This example of visual political satire suggests the publisher and his readers had largely accepted the use of traditional Christian imagery for new secular goals.

---

[1] Quoted in Kenneth Silverman, *A Cultural History of the American Revolution* (New York: Columbia University Press, 1987), 298.

[2] Clifford K. Shipton, *Isaiah Thomas: Printer, Patriot and Philanthropist, 1749–1831* (Rochester, NY: Leo Hart, 1948), 19, 28–30; Silverman, *A Cultural History*, 657 n.2.

[3] Clarence Brigham, *Paul Revere's Engravings* (Worcester, MA; 1954; repr. Atheneum, 1969), 106. On *The Royal American Magazine*, see Frank Luther Mott, *A History of American Magazines, 1741–1850* (1930; repr. Cambridge, MA: The Belknap Press of Harvard University Press, 1966), 26, 36–48, 83–86; and Lyon N. Richardson, *A History of Early American Magazines, 1741–1789* (New York: Thomas Nelson and Sons, 1931), 164–236.

[4] Brigham, *Paul Revere's Engravings*, 111–13.

Figure 3.1 Title page, by P. Revere. Ezra Gleason, *The Massachusetts Calendar for 1774* (Boston: I. Thomas).

Courtesy, American Antiquarian Society.

From 1775 to 1800, Isaiah Thomas established himself as the most important American printer and publisher of his generation. At the height of his productivity, he had sixteen presses in operation, seven of which were in Worcester. His undertakings included papermaking, printing, binding, and delivery, and he had branches under his control in other towns as well. He was the first printer to introduce networks combining printing and bookselling into New England.

Thomas printed almanacs, chapbooks, children's books, spellers, dictionaries, grammars, geographies, army regulations, musical scores, novels, poetry, classical works, Bibles, and magazines, as well as volumes of divinity, medicine, history, biography, and travel.[5] Of the almost nine hundred imprints turned out by his presses, approximately ten percent contain copperplate engravings, and twenty-five percent include wood or metal cuts. Data drawn from the North American Imprint Program (NAIP), a cataloging project of the American Antiquarian Society, indicates that ten percent of all eighteenth-century American imprints were illustrated, and that the illustrations were usually wood or metal cuts, although toward the end of the century, engravings occurred more often. Thomas's imprints parallel those of other publishers with respect to numbers of engravings, but exceed the average for cuts. For the purpose of the present study, illustrated imprints of Isaiah for the period from 1775 to 1800 will be considered categorically, with examples from five areas: children's books, geographies, fiction, *The Massachusetts Magazine*, and the Bible. In the process of organizing his business, Thomas was transformed from an amateur producer of cuts to a committed patron of the illustrative arts.

---

[5] Charles Lemuel Nichols, *Isaiah Thomas: Printer, Writer and Collector* (1912; repr. New York: Burt Franklin, 1967), 27; Richard C. Steele, *Isaiah Thomas* (Worcester, MA: Worcester Telegram and Gazette, Inc. and Worcester Historical Museum, 1981), 24; specific titles are listed in the Isaiah Thomas Papers, AAS, uncataloged material, Account of Stock, April 1796, Box 8.

4

Children's Books

F or some scholars, the most enduring books published by Thomas are the works meant to appeal to children, including alphabet books, riddle books, poems, stories, songs, and hymnals, for which he had a total of 1,500 cuts in stock.[1] Based on "the English plan" of British printer John Newbery, these little volumes embodied the aims and methods of John Locke, who recommended the use of picture books as a study aid, and endorsed works, such as Aesop's *Fables*, as both pleasurable and desirable reading for children. Although virtue, according to Locke, was still the first aim of juvenile reading, he sought to give moral instruction with "innocent amusement," laying down rules for making children healthy, virtuous, and happy.[2]

A work that combines the new principle of amusement for children with the old Puritan concern for spiritual preparation is *A Curious Hieroglyphic Bible*, published by Thomas in 1788 with nearly five hundred cuts. Advertised as "an easy way of leading them [children] on in Reading" and as an effective, playful means of teaching Scripture to the young, each page contains a Biblical quotation in which key words are replaced by pictures of the objects that the words signify. For example, the picture of a sturdy vessel replaces the word "ark" in the passage concerning Noah related in Genesis 8:10–11 (Figure 4.1). The task of deciphering the puzzle was made easy for the reader, if necessary, by referring to the key below. Sentences that explain the figures are placed at the bottom of each page, and the words represented by the figures are identified in italic print. Thomas based his edition on the English hieroglyphic version published in London by T. Hodgson in 1780. The hieroglyphic Bible encompasses a tradition of image and text that flourished on the continent and in England for over a century, the first known example of which was published in Augsburg by Melchior Mattsperger in 1687.[3]

---

[1] Thomas itemizes 56 children's book titles and refers to "several others," all with cuts, printed chiefly in 1787 and 1788; the list is printed in Charles Lemuel Nichols, *Isaiah Thomas: Printer, Writer and Collector* (1912; repr. New York: Burt Franklin, 1967), 132–33. A List of Stock for 1796, including 52 juvenile titles, is printed in Clifford K. Shipton, *Isaiah Thomas: Printer, Patriot and Philanthropist, 1749–1831* (Rochester, NY: Leo Hart, 1948), 86–90.

[2] Monica Kiefer, *American Children Through Their Books, 1700–1835* (Philadelphia: University of Pennsylvania Press, 1948), 12–14; James Axtell, *The Educational Writings of John Locke* (Cambridge: Cambridge University Press, 1968), 259–62; Samuel F. Pickering, Jr., *John Locke and Children's Books in Eighteenth-Century England* (Knoxville: The University of Tennessee Press, 1981).

[3] John T. Irwin, *American Hieroglyphics: The Symbol of the Egyptian Hieroglyphics in the American Renaissance* (New Haven, CT: Yale University Press, 1980), 26–31.

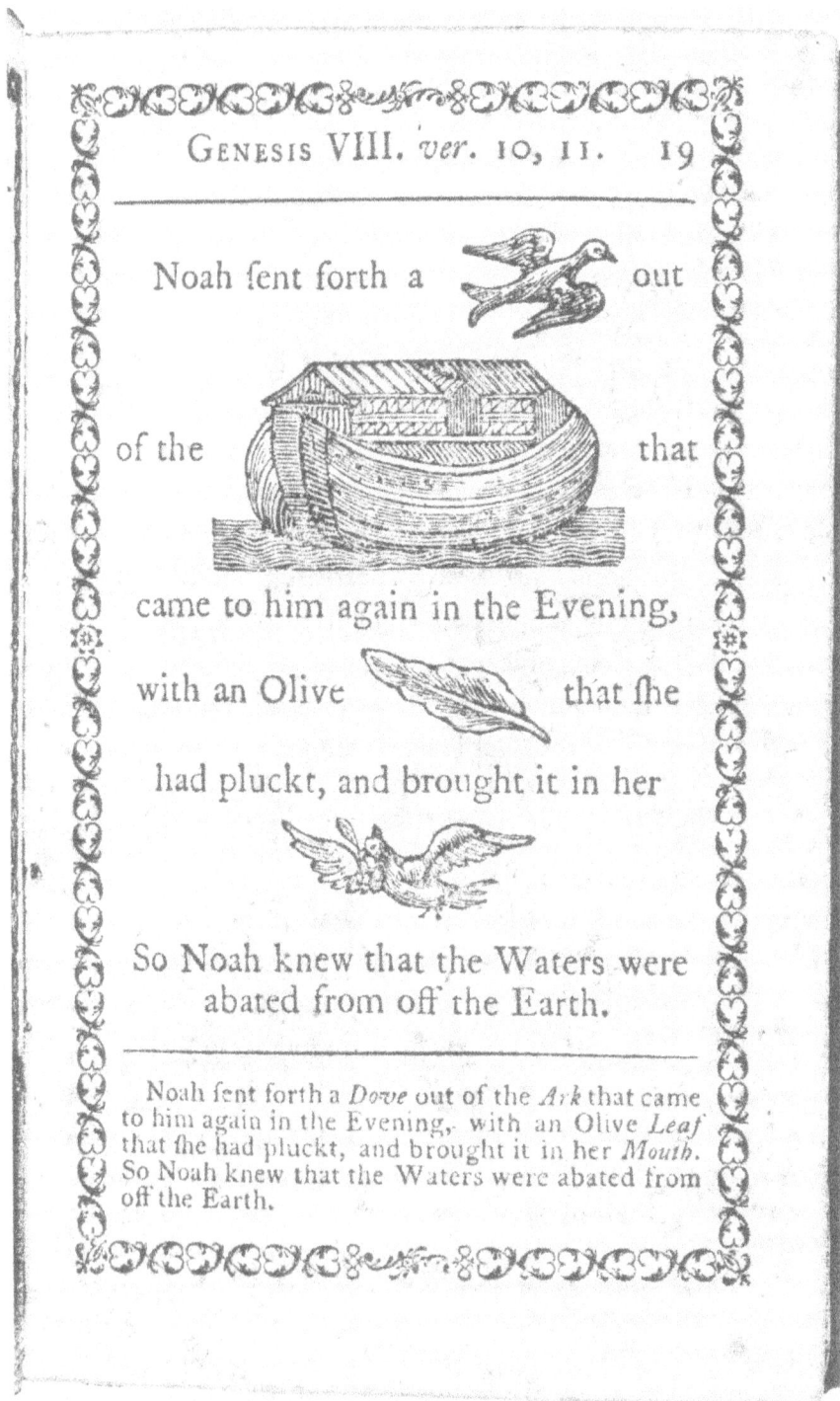

Figure 4.1 *Noah's Ark*, artist unknown. *A Curious Hierogylyphic Bible* (Worcester, MA: I. Thomas, 1788), 19.

Courtesy, American Antiquarian Society.

The more secular examples of children's books produced by Thomas have been credited by scholars with having "lifted the gloom from the nursery," and blending amusement with instruction in a form that was both appealing and marketable. Instead of directing children to read godly books and be mindful of the last judgment, children were increasingly counseled to be virtuous because such conduct led to a successful life on earth. *The Little Pretty Pocket Book*, based on the Newbery edition, issued by Thomas in 1787, is typical of the new attempt to amuse children and put Locke's theories into practice by means of special books. Tiny in format and printed in small type, the size was convenient for children to handle. Although the illustrations at the top of the page were highly simplified and lacked depth, they were numerous and a distinct novelty. A page with "Rules for "Behavior" offers a diminutive illustration in the horizontal oval usually associated with the work by English engraver Thomas Bewick. By depicting boys sharing toys, the image gives the viewer a glimpse into the world of order and amusement recommended for young readers.

However, the entertainment in this type of book is only occasional, often obscured by the maxims or morals attached to the tale. For example, in an illustration for Mary Jane Kilner's *The Adventures of a Pincushion: Designed Chiefly for the Use of Young Ladies,* a mother is admonishing one of her daughters for selfish behavior (Figure 4.2). The emphasis on manners, and the inclusion of an ornate mirror in the room, signals the middle-class preoccupation with refinement, success, and moral certainties. Moreover, the subject of the cut, a woman and two children grouped together, is generic and might be brought into service in similar books, because its lack of individuality was a way of depicting any child's world in simple and uncomplicated terms that could be easily understood. This story, and others written by Mary Jane and Dorothy Kilner, were among the most popular of the late Newbery books. The fine illustrations in the English edition are attributed to John Bewick; the individual who cut

PINCUSHION.   14

difpleafed with you, and the threat you made of breaking her plates in return, is fo very naughty and wicked, that I think you deferve to be punifhed ; and I defire you will afk *Martha's* pardon for the blow you have given her." *Charlotte* coloured with indignation and anger, at the thoughts of fubmitting in fuch a manner to humble herfclf. She had heard fome filly girls declare, they would never confefs to be wrong, and was withheld from acting in the nobleft manner, by the falfe fhame of confeffing an errour. At length, however, upon her Mamma's coming towards her with an a-

vowed

Figure 4.2 [Mary Jane Kilner]. *The Adventures of a Pincushion: Designed Chiefly for the Use of Young Ladies*, artist unknown (Worcester, MA: I. Thomas, 1788), 11.
Courtesy, American Antiquarian Society.

the American illustrations, which closely follow the English originals, is unknown.[4]

The unusual narrator for the text, a pincushion stitched by the young ladies, is an example of what one scholar calls, "a boom in mid-century novels narrated by non-human subjects and inanimate objects."[5] The eighteenth century's fascination with material culture and the material permeability of social class (objects moved where people could not), made stories more attractive when related from the point of view of an "it-narrator." Such tales—told in the voice of a pin, atom, hackney-coach, flea, banknote, or pincushion—may be considered a subcategory of eighteenth-century literature.

Mother Goose's Melody, first published in America by Thomas in 1794, is another example of reproductions by Thomas of English children's books. The idea of editing old nursery rhymes originated about 1760 with Newbery, assisted by Oliver Goldsmith, who worked for him as a hack writer.[6] An unsigned woodcut illustration accompanies each lullaby and song. The cut of two kissing blackbirds, disproportionately large compared to the knoll, house, and trees, nevertheless has warmth and charm (Figure 4.3). Neither publisher nor reader is likely to have been troubled by the lack of perspective, scale, or detail in the illustrations for juvenile imprints. The images of women and children in these late eighteenth-century books give secularized versions of role prescription, if compared to the earlier *History of the Holy Jesus* and *The Prodigal Daughter*, though they did not completely displace these older republished religious works.

---

[4] A. S. N. Rosenbach, *Early American Children's Books* (Portland, Maine, 1933; repr. New York: Kraus Reprint Corp., 1966), No. 131; see also Victor E. Neuburg, *Chapbooks: A Bibliography of References in English and American Chapbook Literature of the 18th and 19th Centuries* (London: Vine Press, 1964); May F. Thwaite, *From Primer to Pleasure in Reading* (Boston: The Horn Book, 1963); and Rosalie V. Halsey, *Forgotten Books of the American Nursery* (1911; Detroit: Singing Tree Press, 1969).

[5] Janine Barchas, *Graphic Design, Print Culture, and the Eighteenth-Century Century Novel* (Cambridge: Cambridge University Press, 2003), 50.

[6] Kiefer, *American Children*, 13.

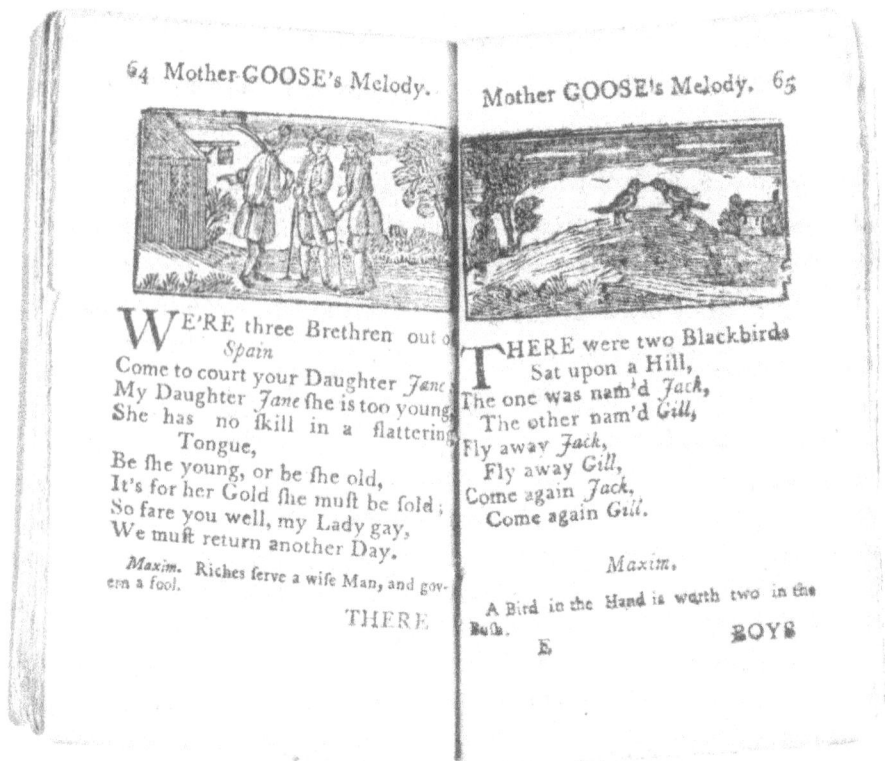

64 Mother GOOSE's Melody.

Mother GOOSE's Melody. 65

WE'RE three Brethren out of
    Spain
Come to court your Daughter Jane;
My Daughter Jane she is too young,
She has no skill in a flattering
        Tongue,
Be she young, or be she old,
It's for her Gold she must be sold;
So fare you well, my Lady gay,
We must return another Day.

  Maxim. Riches serve a wise Man, and gov-
ern a fool.

                    THERE

THERE were two Blackbirds
        Sat upon a Hill,
The one was nam'd Jack,
    The other nam'd Gill,
Fly away Jack,
    Fly away Gill,
Come again Jack,
    Come again Gill.

                Maxim.

  A Bird in the Hand is worth two in the
Bush.
            E.   BOYS

Figure 4.3 *Mother Goose's Melody*, artist unknown (Worcester, MA: I. Thomas, 1794), 64–65.

Courtesy, American Antiquarian Society.

5

Geographies and Their Financial Arrangements

I saiah Thomas published numerous schoolbooks, including spellers, grammars, dictionaries, and geographies, the latter in editions for both children and adults. His own humble origins and remarkable self-education may have prompted Thomas to help others improve their self-esteem and achieve success in the world.[1] His efforts to bring to press the magisterial *American Universal Geography*, by Jedidiah Morse (1761–1826), may be followed in the Isaiah Thomas manuscript papers, which also illumine the business activities associated with book illustration. Most of Thomas's eighteenth-century correspondence is with Ebenezer Turell Andrews (1766–1851), who was his apprentice for seven years before becoming his partner in 1789.[2] Andrews wrote from the firm's location in Newbury Street, Boston, to Thomas, who was centered in Worcester. Their correspondence on this cartographic project reveals the myriad problems faced by authors and engravers who labored under deadlines and budgets imposed by publishers.

Thomas and Andrews negotiated with Morse for publication of his geographical works because following the American Revolution there was great interest in describing the land that formerly had been seen from a European perspective. Morse's elementary text, *Geography Made Easy* (1784), was the beginning of a more extended effort to gather geographic information suitable for an adult audience. Adopted as a text by many teachers, the Rev. Ezra Stiles, president of Yale, wrote in his diary for April 9, 1789, "This day I have introduced by Mr. Tutor Bidwell Morses Geography to be recited by the Soph. class."[3] Morse's geographies were only below the Bible and Noah Webster's spellers in popularity with Americans.[4]

In preparation for the new work, Morse took a trip to the South looking for first-hand information, but also drew heavily on Jefferson's *Notes on Virginia* (1784), made use of pamphlets and magazine articles, and

---

[1] Cathy N. Davidson, *Revolution and the Word: The Rise of the Novel in America* (New York: Oxford University Press, 1986), 88.

[2] Isaiah Thomas (IT) manuscript papers, Boxes 1–3, American Antiquarian Society (AAS). All subsequent quotations from dated letters are from the IT papers, AAS.

[3] Ezra Stiles, *The Literary Diary of Ezra Stiles, ed. under the authority of the corporation of Yale University, by Franklin Bowditch Dexter* (New York: Charles Scribner's & Sons, 1901), 351; Richard J. Moss, *The Life of Jedidiah Morse: A Station of Peculiar Exposure* (Knoxville: The University of Tennessee Press, 1995).

[4] Martin Bruckner, "Lessons in Geography: Maps, Spellers, and Other Grammars of Nationalism in the Early Republic," *American Quarterly* 51 (June 1999), 320.

circulated questionnaires. *The American Geography* of 1789 had been generally well received and sold well, but critics found errors and short-comings, particularly with the maps, which one reader described as "greatly faulty."[5] Thomas began preparations for a more extensive version, entitled *The American Universal Geography*, based on Morse's revisions and new material. He gave more thought to the map problem, and in addition to those maps engraved by Amos Doolittle and Joel Knott Allen, he secured maps of Maine and Pennsylvania made by Osgood Carleton, and a map of the Southern states by Joseph Purcell.[6]

In *The American Universal Geography*, published in 1793, Morse developed a full second volume with maps of Europe and the eastern hemisphere. He proposed "a new world order by starting with a description of the United States *before* delineating Europe, Africa, and Asia," thus "forcing his audience to situate . . . themselves in relation to the world through an America-centric perspective."[7] This edition included a map of the world, drawn "from the best authorities," and engraved by Amos Doolittle, one of the earliest engravers on copper (Figure 5.1). It was not a Mercator projection, with straight lines of longitude and latitude intersecting at right angles, as can be found in his *American Geography* of 1795, but a more visually accurate projection, as developed by Johann Lambert in 1772, in which only the equator and the central meridian are straight lines, and all others are curved, as on a sphere.[8]

The 1793 edition benefited from Morse's involvement with Isaiah Thomas, who printed the work. However, although Thomas and his partner, Andrews, were greatly interested in the possibilities of this project, they took a dislike to Morse for his close attention to the financial arrangements, and were critical of Doolittle's slow execution of the plates as well.

Thomas tried to drive a hard bargain with Morse, writing him that "I must be furnished with copies of all the Maps, before I can make a

---

[5] Hazard and Elkanah Watson to Morse, as quoted in Ralph H. Brown, "The American Geographies of Jedidiah Morse," *Annals of the Association of American Geographers* 31 (September 1941): 175.

[6] For the implications of territorial expansion on early maps, see Laurence M. Hauptman, "Westward the Course of Empire: 1783–1893," *The Historian: A Journal of History* 40 (May 1978): 423–40, and Bruckner, "Lessons in Geography," 311–44.

[7] Bruckner, "Lessons in Geography," 326.

[8] Peter H. Dana, The Geographer's Craft Project, Department of Geography, The University of Colorado at Boulder.

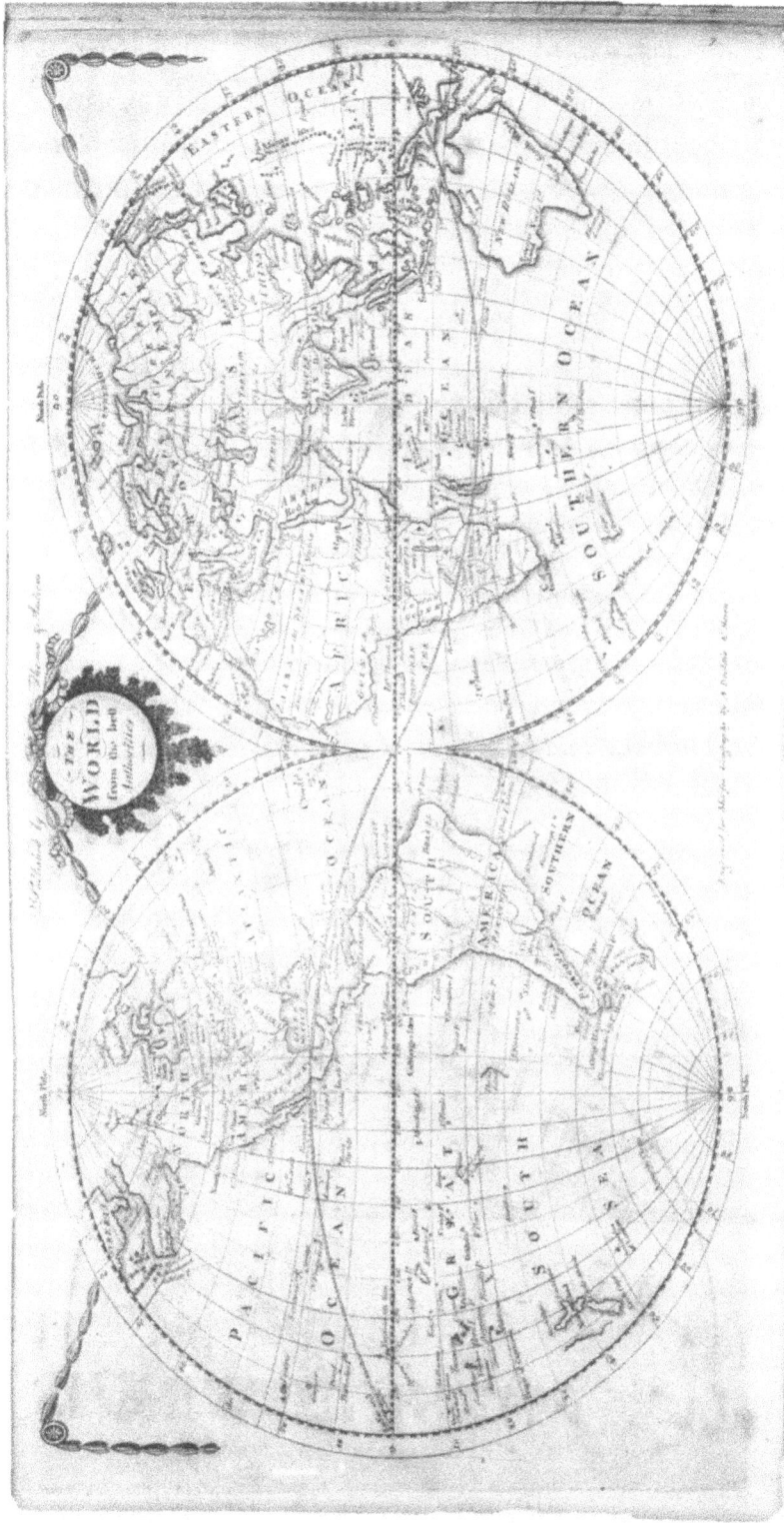

Figure 5.1 *Eastern and Western Hemisphere, Map of the World,* by A. Doolittle. Jedidiah Morse, *The American Universal Geography* (Boston: Thomas and Andrews, 1793), 2 vols.
Courtesy, American Antiquarian Society.

contract for the Engraving of them . . . beg you to get them ready as soon as possible . . . and wish you to be contented with less profit" (March 24, 1793). Andrews, for his part, was still considering less expensive alternatives to Doolittle, but by September, it is evident that Doolittle was given the contract for the geography, and was expected to produce copies from engraved plates as quickly as possible, though further delays ensued.

Despite evidence of recriminations, hurried work, and bargaining about price, the Thomas–Andrews correspondence reveals that all those involved were aware of the significance of *The American Universal Geography*, and expected accuracy, expert craftsmanship, and substantial profit from the volume. Following the publication of Morse's geography, Doolittle's map reached thousands of students over a succession of generations, encouraging allegiance to American interests. The map was instrumental in translating "the rhetoric of nationalism into a perceptible, tangible form that connected the Vermont lawyer, and the Connecticut farmer, the New England statesman and the Southern schoolgirl."[9] Thomas's role in the production of book and map made a notable contribution to the self-fashioning and identity of the new nation.

---

[9]Bruckner, "Lessons in Geography," 317.

6

Novels and Poetry

T homas's vision of an American nation included a desire to encourage American arts and letters, yet, paradoxically, he based them on the British model. He published fiction and verse by some of the major authors of his day, including American writers William Hill Brown and Mercy Otis Warren, as well as English authors Lawrence Sterne, Henry Fielding, and Samuel Richardson. A brief look at illustrations associated with two examples in this genre will indicate the complexity and interest of image and text, and suggest the overlay of British and American literary forms.

Thomas published William Hill Brown's epistolary novel, *The Power of Sympathy*, in 1789. Generally accepted as the "first American novel," it was a major cultural landmark of the early republic. Although not immediately a best seller, its publication marks the recognition of the growing popularity of novel reading in America. *The Power of Sympathy* ostensibly connects extreme sensibility with the social and moral principles underlying Republican virtue, but fascinated the reader with its melodramatic style and plot involving incest and suicide. It has been described aptly as "a didactic essay and a novel . . . shuffled together and bound as a book."[1]

The main plot deals with the imminent incestuous marriage of Harrington and Harriot, who, they learn, are both children of the elder Harrington, one by his marriage and the second by his mistress. When the relationship is discovered, Harriot dies of shock and sadness, and Harrington commits suicide. A subordinate and equally dismal plot deals with the suicide of Orphelia Shepherd after her seduction by her brother-in-law Martin; it parallels the real-life suicide of Sarah Morton's sister after her alleged seduction by Sarah Morton's husband, all members of a prominent Boston family.

Cathy Davidson, in her analysis of the audience for the epistolary novel, sees a gender division among eighteenth-century readers: whereas women were interested in a scandalous story, ironically, men appreciated a didactic novel that promised to edify the female reader. Both readings were

---

[1] Analysis by Leslie Fiedler, in Kenneth Silverman, *A Cultural History of the American Revolution* (New York: Columbia University Press, 1987), 590–91; Cathy N. Davidson, *Revolution and the Word: The Rise of the Novel in America* (New York: Oxford University Press, 1986), 99.

encouraged by the preface, which announced that "the dangerous conse-
quences of seduction are exposed and the advantages of Female Education
set forth and recommended."[2]

The frontispiece (Figure 6.1) by Samuel Hill[3] strongly suggests that
the publisher's intended audience were female readers. Entitled "The
Story of Orphelia," (with the caption, "0 Fatal! Fatal Poison!"), the image
captures the climactic moment of the subplot as the betrayed woman
sinks to the floor, dropping a goblet filled with poison beside her. An
older woman and man, in alarm, rush through the open door to her side,
shocked at her state, but too late to prevent the tragedy. The rich draperies,
ornate mirror and table, and the figured carpet give evidence of the elite
class of the protagonists, while a shaft of light illumines the dark and
fatal scene.

Attracted by the frontispiece, a critical reviewer in *The Massachusetts
Centinel* (Feb. 7, 1789), expressed disappointment that not until the end
did the text fulfill expectations aroused by the illustration. For this reader,
at least, according to Davidson, "the engraving constituted a kind of
covenant between the reader and the text, but one which the text only
minimally honored." The frontispiece, in this case, had not established
the theme of the book, and, the newspaper critic continues, "It is not
until we arrive near the end of the work, that we find anything to authorize
the title." However, another reviewer, Antonia, in *The Herald of Freedom*
(Feb. 10) countered that "the author [of *The Power of Sympathy*] 'merits
the most grateful acknowledgment from our sex,' because of the 'respect
and tenderness' he has shown to 'youthful females.'" Implicit in this
second reading is the view that the moral of the frontispiece indeed was
born out in the text. But at the outset, the printer had made a quite
direct and visual appeal to the reader by placing the word "seduction"
prominently in the front of the book. This key word is centered on the
dedication page, occupies an entire line, and is printed in large, bold,
capitalized letters.[4]

---

[2] Davidson, *Revolution and the Word*, 97–98.

[3] Sinclair H. Hitchings, Samuel Hill's Relief Engraving," *Printing and Graphic Arts* 8 (March 1960): 12–20.

[4] Davidson, *Revolution and the Word*, 91, 96–97. On women's education and reading, see also Linda Kerber, *Women of the Republic: Intellect and Ideology in Revolutionary America* (Chapel Hill: University of North Carolina Press, 1980), 185–264.

Figure 6.1 Frontispiece, *The Story of Orphelia*, by S. Hill. *The Power of Sympathy* (Boston: I. Thomas, 1789).

Courtesy, American Antiquarian Society.

A taste for elegance in printed fiction and a desire for its prestige prompted Thomas and Andrews to plan for the publication of Charlotte Smith's *Sonnets,* a work "of great merit," argued Andrews, "printed by [English publisher John] Bell in his stile of printing, adorned with . . . 3 elegant copperplates. My wish is to do them in every respect equal to the copy." Joseph Seymour, the engraver finally chosen for this work, submitted sketches for Thomas's approval before they were engraved (Sept. 28, 1792). The first Worcester edition was based on the sixth London edition, with added material.

Though the plates for this work were executed promptly, Thomas delayed publication for four years because, as he explained in an advertisement accompanying Smith's *Elegiac Sonnets,* he was engaged in other projects that had tied up his stock of type. He regretted that the plates for this work had been engraved earlier, because given "the infancy of engraving in this country, four years' additional experience to the artist [Joseph Seymour] would doubtless have produced more delicate work than what is now presented." Thomas continues in an apologetic tone: "The Editor doubts not but a proper allowance will be made for work engraved by an artist who obtained his knowledge in this country, by whom these plates were executed, and that done by European engravers who have settled in the United States." In a bid for approval, Thomas "hopes for the candor of those who wish well to the production of the Columbia [American] press—their favorable acceptance of this, and other volumes printed in this country, will doubtless raise an emulation to produce others, better executed, on superior paper, and with more delicate engravings" (Oct. 1795).

The judgment of the engravings by Thomas is modest and accurate. Each simple engraving in the book is presented in an oval shape, set against a rectangular ruled background, and topped with a garland beneath which a dramatic figure poses in a shallow landscape (Figure 6.2). The author, Charlotte Smith [1749–1806], had given instructions to the binder of her book to "Let the plates face the Sonnets to which they belong, though "the reader will note this plate [the frontispiece] belongs to the elegy page 83."[5] The frontispiece depicts a woman on her knees, with

---

[5] Charlotte Turner Smith, *Elegiac Sonnets* (Worcester, MA, 1791). This first Worcester edition was based on the sixth London edition, with added material. Miscellaneous front matter, not paginated, includes "Directions to the Binder" about how to place the plates.

Dark gathering clouds involve &c.

Figure 6.2 Frontispiece, by J. Seymour. Charlotte Smith, *Elegiac Sonnets* (Worcester, MA: I. Thomas, 1795).

Courtesy, American Antiquarian Society.

left arm raised, posed beneath a looming sky. Below the image, a fragment of verse written in graceful script, "Dark gath'ring clouds involved etc.," refers to a line from the associated text. It prepares the reader for a stanza of mournful grief over a lover lost at sea: "Thus with clasp'd hands, wild looks and streamy hair,/While shrieks of horror broke her trembly speech,/ A wretched maid—the victim of Despair/Survey'd the threat'ning storm and desert beech."

The illustrations in the *Sonnets* have been largely ignored by viewers, in contrast to the positive response to the poetry by readers and critics when initially published. Other verses and novels by Smith also express in melancholy tones her personal sorrow in an unhappy marriage, appreciative feelings for natural scenery, and compassion for the poor and oppressed. Although Smith's work initially received a popular reception, interest waned over time. More recently, renewed attention has been given by scholars who suggest her writings added to the development of a sentimental tradition that valued women of intelligence, creativity, grace, and sensitivity.[6]

At the height of Smith's popularity, one American reader expressed appreciation to Thomas for a gift of the illustrated work; Thad. M. Harris of Dorchester writes his thanks "for the elegant present of Miss Smith's Sonnets & the Grammar & Almanac accompanying. I need not repeat to you my opinion of the beauty of impression of the former" (Jan. 7, 1797). Harris's response was not unique, and these literary and artistic endeavors speak to the growth of polite arts and learning in which Thomas, as publisher, was engaged. Thomas's introduction to the *Sonnets* shows his veiled pride in creating this American product: the finest type, paper, engravings, and bindings.

---

[6]Elizabeth R. Napier, "Charlotte Smith, 1749–1806," *British Novelists, 1660–1800*, Part 2: M–Z, ed. Martin Battestin, *Dictionary of Literary Biography* 39 (Detroit: Gale Research Co., 1985), 433–40; Jane Spencer, "Charlotte Smith," in *The Rise of the Woman Novelist: From Aphra Behn to Jane Austen* (Totowa, NJ: Rowman & Allanheld, 1985), 287–89.

7

The Massachusetts Magazine

Polite letters played an important role in the development of a new magazine undertaken by Thomas. Success seemed assured because he already had experience with publishing *The Royal American Magazine* and *The Worcester Magazine*.[1] A lengthy literary proposal set forth the reasons for publishing *The Massachusetts Magazine,* arguing that there was nothing similar in the state, friends were encouraging the plan, and the company was equipped for the project. Copperplate engravings and sheet music were emphasized as costly but desirable features. Literary content consisted of sentimental fiction (such as installments of *The Power of Sympathy*), poetry, biography, history, congressional news, and essay serials.[2] Thomas hoped for a general audience as well as support from the elite. To attract "men of learning," he would publish a wide array of articles on the arts and sciences, but he also wanted "to cultivate the friendship of the Virtuous Fair—they are entitled to a full share of our rational amusement." Thomas was aware of a growing number of women readers who were increasing the demand for books that educated and entertained across the spectrum of class, gender, and generational lines.[3]

The Massachusetts Magazine intended to include with each issue a frontispiece copperplate engraving on domestic subjects "as being more agreeable to the citizens of the new Empire, than copying sketches from European masters"; about half of the engravings eventually produced were on American subjects. Samuel Hill engraved the signed plates for the magazine from 1789 to 1796, and may have executed the unsigned ones as well.[4] At the end of 1791, perhaps to cut costs, an editorial announcement proposed to "furnish eight pages of good Letter Press in lieu of each engraving," and to abandon "the trivial decoration of a plate, which only amuses the eye, without informing the mind, or meliorating

---

[1] After the state legislature passed an Act taxing newspaper advertisements, reminiscent to Thomas of the hated Stamp Act, he suspended *The Massachusetts Spy,* and for two years turned it into the format of an octavo magazine, *The Worcester Magazine,* not subject to the duty, though concerned with the political and economic issues of the day; Lyon N. Richardson, *A History of Early American Magazines, 1741–1789* (New York: Thomas Nelson and Sons, 1931), 258–59.

[2] Ibid., 354–61.

[3] Cathy N. Davidson, *Revolution and the Word: The Rise of the Novel in America* (New York: Oxford University Press, 1986), 55–79.

[4] Benjamin M. Lewis, "Engravings in American Magazines, 1741–1810," in *Books in America's Past,* ed. David Kaser (Charlottesville: University Press of Virginia, 1966), 204–17.

the heart." But readers objected and the plates were restored.[5] Two illustrations, one portraying landscape, the other an urban view, produced for *The Massachusetts Magazine* when under the management of Isaiah Thomas are of particular interest and will be considered in some detail.

Landscape accounted for about one quarter of illustrations in all magazines, and editors frequently made public appeals for original sketches and ideas for plates; they asked also for written descriptions of the views to provide context. These texts were meant to be subordinate to the images, and generally appeared on the facing page. More amateurs than professional artists provided designs, but the plates were cut by engravers retained by the magazines on a regular basis. Like other editors of magazines, Thomas made an effort to draw on readers' willingness to associate American landscape with a common identity, and to help define the new national unity in visual terms.[6]

The November 1790 issue of *The Massachusetts Magazine* carried the frontispiece, *S.E. Prospect, from an Eminence near the Common, Boston* (Figure 7.1). When readers view the engraving, they first focus on the foreground, which shows a visitor who has dismounted from his horse, is accompanied by his dog, and directs our gaze. We next glance down a rocky hill, past a centrally located solitary tree, halt briefly at a fenced pasture, and move on to a crowded slip of land, beyond which is a row of ship's masts, another stretch of water, and a series of sparsely wooded but monumental hills on the horizon. With bold, straightforward composition and simple draftsmanship, the artist has portrayed a vernacular landscape; neat, cheerful artifacts of workmanship—houses, ships, cleared fields—exemplifying a cultivated vista tucked between two impressive rows of hills. The illustration gives evidence of productive occupation and domestication, and contrasts commerce and agriculture, but it is also a realistic transcription of topography. The "Description of the Plate" identifies the landmarks, associates them with an important Revolutionary War battle, and encourages aesthetic appreciation of their beauty:

> The rising ground, from which the accompanying prospect was taken, is situated near Governour Hancock's mansion house; and commands a beauti-

---

[5] Preface to vol. III issued with the number for Dec. 1791; Frank Luther Mott, *A History of American Magazines, 1741–1850* (1930; repr. Cambridge, MA: The Belknap Press of Harvard University Press, 1966), 110.

[6] Karol Ann Peard Lawson, "An Inexhaustible Abundance: The National Landscape Depicted in American Magazines, 1790–1820," *Journal of the Early Republic* 12 (Fall 1992): 307–10.

Figure 7.1 Frontispiece, *Prospect . . . Near the Common*, by S. Hill. *Massachusetts Magazine* (Nov. 1790).

Courtesy, American Antiquarian Society.

ful view of the South East of Boston, with a vast extend of private and public buildings, wharfs, shipping and water. At a distance are seen, the memorable heights of Dorchester, whose formidable appearance in 1776, discomposed the military nerves of Britain; and eventually necessitate a retreat from the capitol of Massachusetts. The great variety of objects, that croud upon the point of vision, are too numerous for detail—suffice it to observe, that the busy din of the town, and the quiet stillness of the rural hamlet, appear in striking contrast, and furnish a luxuriant feast, to the contemplative and philosophick mind.

According to Albert Boime, the viewpoint is characteristic of early American landscape representations: a visual trajectory from the uplands to a scenic panorama below. "[S]uch a composition is arranged with the spectator in mind, either assuming the elevated viewpoint of the onlooker or including a staffage figure seen from behind that functions as a surrogate onlooking." The prospect incorporates the past, present, and future of the landscape, and implicitly reveals the emerging idea of American "manifest destiny" and unlimited growth.[7]

The second illustration from *The Massachusetts Magazine* to be considered is a scene of the heart of Boston, drawn and engraved by Samuel

---

[7] Albert Boime, *The Magisterial Gaze* (Washington, DC: Smithsonian Institution Press, 1991), 1.

Figure 7.2 Frontispiece, *View of the State House, Boston*, by S. Hill. *Massachusetts Magazine* (July 1793).
Courtesy, American Antiquarian Society.

Hill. Early views of American cities usually emphasized commercial features that imposed order on nature, and were derived essentially from the English picturesque tradition.[8] Pastoral conventions served to conceal the unpleasant effects of industrialization in urban views even into the nineteenth century. Although depictions of American city streets did not appear until the end of the eighteenth century, they too were dependent on European pictorial tradition, highlighting the positive aspects of street life. The chaotic activity in city streets was not depicted in the popular press until the nineteenth century.

"View of the State House, in Boston," published in July 1793, shows the State House flanked by warehouses and shops (Figure 7.2). The

---

[8] For examples of the tradition, see E. McSherry Fowble, *Two Centuries of Prints in America, 1680–1880: A Selective Catalogue of the Winterthur Museum Collection* (Charlottesville: University Press of Virginia, 1987); and Lynn Glaser, *Engraved America: Iconography of America Through 1800* (Philadelphia: Ancient Orb Press, 1970).

central building is rich with architectural detail, including a graceful steeple with quoins, gabled windows, a column and pedimented doorway, and a stately progression of windows along the side of the structure. This South West view, according to the "Description of the Plate" as prepared by the editors, "also exhibits several capital buildings improved by merchants of eminence." Furthermore,

> The busy scenes of life which are daily acting on this popular theatre of general resort, are strongly delineated by the various groups of industrious citizens passing to and fro, on horseback, afoot, or in carriages. The shipping, discovered at a distance, whose towering masts appear like a rising forest, has a peculiarly fine effect; and the *tout ensemble* forms the finest view that we have ever offered to our generous patrons.

Although the editorial comment emphasizes the compositional skill of the engraver in combining creativity with utility in this urban view, such prints were popular images, and as such, were less influenced by the engraver's aesthetic sense than by the concerns of both artist and publisher to satisfy public taste in order to ensure commercial success through quantity sales.[9]

The Thomas–Andrews correspondence documents a disorderly business, involving decisions made on the basis of intuition, calculated advantages taken of competitors and suppliers, books and newspapers lost or rummaged in transit, and payments to creditors interminably delayed. It is difficult to imagine how any edition of a work was assembled without omissions or errors in pagination. In spite of the chaos, the partnership was extraordinarily successful, as is evident in Andrews's delighted boast on July 16, 1793: "Enclosed you have a statement of our Company Business. . . . The balance, I think will greatly exceed your expectation—it certainly goes beyond my most Sanguine hopes." Some operations undoubtedly were more profitable than others; several months earlier, Andrews had made an effort to discontinue publication of *The Massachusetts Magazine* because it did not pay. He noted, "[I]n addition to the expense and trouble, there is sending them out, and drawing and sending out arts, which is a very considerable job" (Nov. 3, 1792). A year later, the partners disposed of the magazine to two printers and the engraver

[9] Fowble, *Two Centuries of Prints*, xii.

Hill, perhaps because the venture was unprofitable, or perhaps as a first step by Thomas toward simplifying his complex business enterprises.[10] The magazine ultimately was not an economic success, laboring under high production costs, a limited market, and competition from English magazines. Nevertheless, the varied format and length of life was notable for the time. Its grandiose ambition was to bring uplift and refinement to America, or, as stated by the editor, to "improve the taste, the language, and the manners of the age."[11]

[10] Frank Luther Mott, *Golden Multitudes: The Story of Best Sellers in the United States* (New York: Bowker, 1947), 108–11; Richard C. Steele, *Isaiah Thomas* (Worcester, MA: Worcester Telegram and Gazette, Inc. and Worcester Historical Museum, 1981), 26.

[11] Quoted by Davidson, *Revolution and the Word*, 88.

8

The *Holy Bible* of 1791

The publishing project that was dearest to Thomas's heart, the work on which he staked his claim for reputation, was a full-text, lavishly illustrated edition of the Bible, printed in folio and royal quarto; it is the only work he describes in his *History of Printing in America* as a product of his press in Worcester. Subsequently, Benjamin Franklin would praise Thomas as "the Baskerville of America," comparing Thomas to John Baskerville, whose Bible printed in 1763 was considered the finest book produced in England up to that time.[1]

In the first pages of the Bible, Thomas describes the sources used and care taken in producing his text. Before printing, every page was examined by the Worcester clergy, and compared with eight editions, as well as with the editor's own extensive collection of Bibles, including the celebrated Bishop Cranmer's translation of 1540. "In cases of difference," Thomas states, "the preference has been given to the most ancient British copies of the present [King James's] translation, when there was good evidence that these were correct."[2] Thomas, therefore, was the editor as well as the printer of this outstanding Bible.

A promotional prospectus issued for the quarto announced his ambitious intent. "Search the Scripture for there are contained the Words of Eternal Life! They have God for their Author! Salvation for their End!— And Truth unmixed with Error for their Matter." Intended for "Christians of Every Denomination," the "noble object" of the Bible was to bring about "the supreme and ultimate happiness of men," and therefore it was necessary to support the good work by subscribing to one or more copies.

---

[1] Bruce Metzger of Princeton Theological Seminary called Thomas "a learned printer," one who had made "an unsung contribution to Biblical scholarship"; *Journal of Religion* (October 1952): 254–62. Isaiah Thomas, *The History of Printing in America*, 2 vols. (Albany, NY: 1874; repr. New York: Burt Franklin, 1971), lxxvii. A recent study of early American religious imagery is provided by Paul C. Gutjahr, *An American Bible: A History of the Good Book in the United States, 1770–1880* (Stanford: Stanford University Press, 1988). See also P. Marion Simms, *The Bible in America: Versions That Have Played Their Part in the Making of the Republic* (New York: Wilson-Erickson, 1936); Ruth B. Bottigheimer, *Children's Bibles: Sacred Stories, Eternal Words, and Holy Pictures* (Cambridge, MA: Houghton Library, 1994); Ernest S. Frerichs, ed. *The Bible and Bibles in America* (Atlanta: Scholars Press, 1988); and Margaret T. Hills, ed. *The English Bible in America. A Bibliography of Editions ... 1777–1957* (New York: American Bible Society, 1961). The following discussion of artistic sources for the Bible illustrations is drawn from my work, *From Sacred to Secular: Visual Images in Early American Publications* (Newark: University of Delaware Press, 2007).

[2] An address "To Christians of Every Denomination" was published in 1791 in the front unnumbered pages of the royal quarto and folio editions, and is reprinted in John Wright, *Early Bibles of America* (New York: Thomas Whittaker, 1894), 83–84.

Fifty copperplate engravings, based on subjects in both the Hebrew scriptures and the New Testament, are distributed throughout the volumes. In many religious books by the 1790s, illustrations had increased substantially, not only because the old prohibition about "graven images" was on the wane, but because of technological improvements, commercial developments in the manufacture of books, and increased sales. One agent seeking subscriptions for the Thomas Bible in Portland described the attraction: "{I]f you will excuse me, I will give you one word of advice, never print a bible, without pictures, they are somewhat novel in this country, and have a wonderful *effect* upon the nerves and optics of Yankees!!!"[3] Thomas also was aware of the visual appeal, as when he wrote a Philadelphia printer to whom he had sent the Bible in sheets: "By accident I am led to doubt whether I sent you the two frontispieces for the Quarto Bible.—If I have not, I wish you to inform me immediately that I may send them on, as I would by no means have the Books bound up without them."[4]

Yet not every illustration appealed to every viewer. Andrews wrote to Thomas that "Mr. Belknap [a minister] was in the Store looking at the plates of your bible before they were sent to Convention—he thought the position of the figures in the first plate, especially Eve, whose in a very indecent posture. Wish you to look at it" (May 26, 1791). The plate may or may not have been altered, but it is clear that there were two opposing views of the scantily clad Eve. According to one scholar, although Thomas may have been trying to cultivate a refined European sensibility through the image, Belknap saw it as indecent and inappropriate in a Bible. What was desirable for one spectator in this instance was unacceptable to another.[5] Illustrations may be the response of a particular artist to a selected biblical text, or they may be determined by the publisher's instructions. Readers appear to have reacted variously to these illustrations according to their individual mind-sets.

The conception of the Bible as a panorama of morality plays is sustained by the fifty copperplate engravings included in both the folio and royal quarto editions. The prints were executed by Joseph Seymour, Amos

---

[3] Elijah Kellog, to Isaiah Thomas, Portland, Jan. 20, 1792, Thomas Papers, AAS.
[4] Isaiah Thomas to William Young, Philadelphia, Aug. 22, 1792, Thomas Papers, AAS.
[5] Gutjahr, *American Bible*, 49, 56.

Doolittle, Samuel Hill, and John Norman. Many of the texts chosen from the Old Testament for illustration in this Bible are dramatic and violent, and viewers are not spared the horror of the details, as in the illustration by Seymour for "The Falling Walls of Jericho" (Figure 8.1). Jericho, an ancient Canaanite city, taken by Joshua when he led the children of Israel out of the wilderness and into the Promised Land, was completely destroyed. We are shown partially clad women and children under attack, while a man vainly attempts to protect them from soldiers wielding swords and spears; in the left background, buildings are in flames, while large boulders, some topped by trees, tumble down and create further havoc.

In another instance, the engraving by Samuel Hill for "The Philistines cutting off the Heads of Saul and his Three Sons" shows two trunks of bodies, two severed heads, and a man about to be decapitated. The frame mimics the action; above the Bible illustration one putto is in the act of beheading another, while below the illustration is a medallion with crossed swords and a head on an oval shield. Comparable framing has been described by one scholar as the "margin(al) as supplement and count-ertext," a description that has implications for Hill's Bible illustration: The ferocious devastation and somber mood of the subject matter is undermined by the surrounding frame of chubby winged infants engaged in child's play.[6]

Volume Two, with the Apocrypha and the New Testament, includes a number of more static illustrations in which women are the principal figures, including Queen Esther, Susanna, Mary Magdalene, and Martha. The illustration for Suzanna is by Joseph Seymour (Figure 8.2).

Susanna, wife of a prosperous Jew, is a heroine whose story, set in Babylon during the Exile, tells how the woman was secretly desired by two elders in the community who plan to seduce her at her bath in the garden. Thwarted in their efforts, the men swore she was unfaithful, had her brought to court, and saw that she was condemned to death. The young Daniel came to her rescue by pointing to conflicting evidence and proving Susanna's innocence. The image of Susanna appears in the Christian art of the Roman catacombs, meant to represent a righteous person ultimately delivered from evil. In the Middle Ages, she was the

---

[6] Peter Wagner, *Reading Iconotexts: From Swift to the French Revolution* (London: Reacktion Books, 1995), esp. chap. 3.

Figure 8.1 *The Falling of the Walls of Jericho,* by J. Seymour. *The Holy Bible* (Worcester, MA: I. Thomas, 1791), Vol. I.

Courtesy, American Antiquarian Society.

Figure 8.2 *Susanna*, by J. Seymour. *The Holy Bible* (Worcester, MA: I. Thomas, 1791), Vol. II. Courtesy, American Antiquarian Society.

symbol of the Church menaced, and was shown in the trial scene where she was exonerated, exemplifying legal justice. From the Renaissance onward, the moment chosen for portrayal was Susanna bathing, which provided an opportunity to paint the subject of female nudity. In the Seymour engraving, Susanna, surprised by the leering elders, is depicted partially nude against an elaborate shell-shaped fountain adorned with putti. In this instance, the winged infants feature as the attendants of Cupid, the god of love in antiquity, widely adopted in Hellenistic and Renaissance art, and in later times as well.[7]

Of the thirty-two engravings executed by Joseph Seymour, sixteen are identified by him as being indebted to the work of earlier European artists, including Rubens, Le Moyne, Le Sueur, Metz, Stothard, Harding, Smith, Bloemart, and Guido Reni. Le Sueur and Le Moyne were among those who developed the French neoclassical style, and were influenced by Raphael, master painter of the Italian High Renaissance. An analysis of Seymour's engravings with an indication of their derivation provides insight into the art of illustrating texts as well as other cultural developments in eighteenth-century America.

Seymour's "Crucifixion" (Figure 8.3) is a close copy of a work by Flemish painter Peter Paul Rubens, "Le Coup de Lance" (1620), with the image reversed. In Rubens's Baroque composition, a Roman soldier inflicts the final wound to Christ, whose figure is calm and triumphant at the moment of death, in contrast to the writhing bodies of the thieves, caught while in physical and emotional torment.[8] In Seymour's version, instead of three Marys in the foreground, there are two; the drapery of the man on horseback is not clearly articulated; the bearded soldier on the ladder seems to have the face of a lion; and the contrast of Christ's tranquil expression with the strained faces of the thieves has been muted into indistinguishable, formulaic facial features. Since Seymour did not travel abroad, he must have worked from a sketch or engraving of the Rubens painting. It is not known whether the differences in composition were produced by Seymour or were already present in his source.

---

[7] James Hall, *Dictionary of Subjects & Symbols in Art* (New York: Harper & Row, 1979); on Susanna, see 294; on putto, see 256; on Cupid, see 87; on cherub, see Angel, 16–17.

[8] C. V. Wedgewood, *The World of Rubens, 1577–1640* (New York: Time Life Books, 1967), 52. Irma B. Jaffe, ed., *The Italian Presence in American Art, 1760–1860* (New York: Fordham University Press, 1989); on American interest in the "old masters," see Lillian Miller, *Patrons and Patriotism: The Encouragement of the Fine Arts in the United States, 1790–1860* (Chicago: Chicago University Press, 1966).

Figure 8.3 *Crucifixion*, by J. Seymour, *The Holy Bible* (Worcester, MA: I. Thomas, 1791), Vol. II.
Courtesy, American Antiquarian Society.

Another engraving by Seymour (Figure 8.4) is based on Guido Reni's late Italian Baroque painting of "St. Michael and the Devil" (1636), much admired by Reni's contemporaries for brilliantly juxtaposing the natural and the ethereal.[9] Michael, the guardian angel of the Hebrew nation, was adopted by the medieval Church to explain the essential Christian conflict—Christ versus the Antichrist—in terms of the archangel Michael battling with the devil.[10] In Seymour's engraving, Michael is a handsome young man with wings, clad in armor and holding aloft his drawn sword. His foot tramples down Satan, shown in his semi-human form with a distorted face, struggling as the saint is about to slay him.

The subject of Michael and the Devil was extraordinarily popular in the seventeenth century, Giordano having treated the theme about a dozen times during his career. These Baroque studies harken back to prototypes by Raphael,[11] but so many replicas and copies were produced by artists, their assistants, and their followers that it is difficult, usually impossible, to identify a particular painting or print as a source for a specific work. Because of limited access to Raphael's originals, copies and engravings "after Raphael" became an important source for artists. These works were not exact transcriptions, but rather interpretations of the original, shaped by the artist's preconceptions and values, which tended to emphasize certain aspects and minimize others.[12] For example, Seymour's engraving is similar to the oil painting by Raphael in the arrangement of figures, in the spiraling curls of drapery, and in the conception of the devil as half man and half beast.[13] However, the archangel's face in the Raphael painting has an expression of rarified beauty and sentiment that Seymour's engraving tried to capture, but with less success.

Isaiah Thomas aspired to the ideals achieved by the high Renaissance art of sixteenth-century Italy, whether or not American illustrators were up to such standards. Raphael, the most typical of the Renaissance artists,

---

[9] *The Age of Correggio and the Carracci: Emilian Painting of the Sixteenth and Seventeenth Centuries* (Washington, DC: National Gallery of Art, 1986), 330.

[10] Hall, *Dictionary*, 208.

[11] Stephen Pepper, *A Taste for Angels: Neapolitan Painting in North America, 1650-1750* (New Haven, CT: Yale University Press, 1987), 125.

[12] Martin Rosenberg, *Raphael and France: The Artist as Paradigm and Symbol* (University Park: The Pennsylvania State University Press, 1995), 14.

[13] S. J. Freedberg, *Painting of the High Renaissance in Rome and Florence* (Cambridge, MA: Harvard University Press, 1961).

Figure 8.4 *Michael and the Devil*, by J. Seymour, *The Holy Bible* (Worcester, MA: I. Thomas, 1791), Vol. II.

Courtesy, American Antiquarian Society.

had shown a love of beauty in his compositions, creating balance and harmony by using the forms of classical Greek art. Raphael, Michelangelo, and other contemporary artists held to the neo-Platonic belief that the soul rises to its enlightenment by progressively rarefied experiences of the beautiful. For Isaiah Thomas, to be a champion of Renaissance cultural production was to trumpet to the world that a class of Americans existed who were learned, tasteful, and refined.

9

Conclusion

T he imperfect use of many visual sources by engravers and woodcutters for imprint illustrations parallels what David D. Hall refers to as a "muddied, multilayered process" by which culture was transmitted, preserving and passing along many bits and pieces of past systems of belief.[1] In the "wonder stories" that were imported, colonists read fragments from the classical and early Christian sources, including Vergil and Josephus, medieval chronicles, sixteenth- and seventeenth-century encyclopedias and collections, and John Foxe's *Acts and Monuments* as well as the Bible. Strands of these stories were woven into popular reading in both England and the New England colonies.[2]

Similarly, one can find in the illustrations printed by Isaiah Thomas an eclectic artistic tradition that most Americans could "read" and understand. Remnants may be found of early Christian symbolism, such as angels; medieval morality plays, with the stage figure of the devil; memento mori imagery, including coffins and gravestones; Renaissance paintings, with illustrations "after Raphael"; Baroque Flemish painting and copies of Rubens's work; French neoclassicism, and its revival of Greek and Roman classical architecture; and Rococo motifs, found in partial nudity, putti, and picture framing. The "Old Masters" had many imitators, as well as new creative artists who built on the achievements of their predecessors in Europe and England. Knowledge of these various traditions and how they were used was gained by American engravers and their audiences by means of imported books and prints.

As technology became more sophisticated, and as colonial interest in acquiring engravings and illustrated books grew, American craftsmen began to offer work of their own manufacture as an alternative to English production. Although their first efforts were not impressive compared to foreign accomplishments, they had the advantage of being able to supply local markets quickly. When the manufacture of single-sheet prints in America was slow to take hold, many engravers turned to the production of individual plates for magazines and books as an alternative means

---

[1] David D. Hall, *Worlds of Wonder, Days of Judgment: Popular Religious Belief in Early New England* (New York: Alfred A. Knopf, 1989), 11; similarly, see Peter Burke, *Popular Culture in Early Modern Europe* (London: Temple Smith, 1978), 115.
[2] Hall, *Worlds of Wonder*, 75.

of making a living.[3] Printer and bookseller Isaiah Thomas advertised dozens of American editions, many with illustrations, available to "the friends of Literature, who wish to encourage the Art of Printing in America" (1790).

Historians have pointed out that although the late eighteenth century was a period in which American nationalism developed, it was also an era when an "Atlantic perspective" flourished.[4] Americans bought books with maps and landscape views of their new nation, but drew much of their orientation on these subjects from England. Long derided as "derivative," early American illustrations may now be best understood as part of a transatlantic culture, expressive of multiple strands of the transatlantic experience.[5] According to J. H. Plumb, Americans of the time were "deeply English," in good measure because of the affluence on both sides of the Atlantic and the surge in the size of the middle class in America. As there were never enough skilled American craftsmen to supply the needs of the wealthy, luxury goods were imported. Americans copied or used the British examples in their own productions, as, for example, when Thomas's 1785 specimen book of type proudly announced that his unusually large stock was "Chiefly Manufactured by that great artist, William Caslon, Esq., of London."[6] British culture remained dominant until the early nineteenth century, when American urban centers developed—in literature, painting, and the arts—cultural expression of their own.[7] The illustrated imprints of Isaiah Thomas were on the cusp of this change.

The Isaiah Thomas papers show that in the process of expanding his enterprise, Thomas was transformed from a carver of cuts to a patron of the illustrative arts. He sought to publish works of literature that rivaled fine British editions, but at the same time, he advertised for original

---

[3] See E. McSherry Fowble, *Two Centuries of Prints in America, 1680–1880: A Selective Catalogue of the Winterthur Museum Collection* (Charlottesville: University Press of Virginia, 1987), x.

[4] Bernard Bailyn, *Atlantic History: Concept and Contours* (Cambridge, MA: Harvard University Press, 2005); David D. Hall, "The Atlantic World," in *A History of the Book in America Vol. One: The Colonial Book in the Atlantic World*, eds. Hugh Amory and David D. Hall (Cambridge: Cambridge University Press, 2000).

[5] David Thelen, "The Nation and Beyond: Transnational Perspectives in United States History," *Journal of American History* 86 (December 1999): 965–75.

[6] Amory and Hall, *History of the Book*, I: 170.

[7] J. H. Plumb, "America and England, 1720–1820: The Fusion of Cultures," in *American Art: 1750–1800 Towards Independence* (New Haven, CT: Yale University Art Gallery, 1976), 15–21; and Neil Harris, "The Making of an American Culture: 1750–1800," in *American Art*, 22–31.

American essays and designs. Engravings in his publications were modeled on English and continental examples, and craftsmen from abroad were acknowledged as superior to American workmen, yet, Samuel Hill's engraving of the Boston State House, imbued with joyful creativity, was pronounced by Thomas to be the "finest view" ever offered in his magazine.

Although it has been argued by some scholars that focus on the visual is the mark of a modern period, and represents a radical break with the essentially textual approach to learning in earlier times, others see this as a mistaken notion. W. J. T. Mitchell goes so far as to say there always has been an "inextricable weaving together of representation and discourse" with images. New media, such as photographs, video, and digital imagery, which seem obsessed with the visual, are actually very similar to visual productions in the past, in that both are not accurate representations of truth, but, instead, are highly constructed versions of reality. Furthermore, in this view, traditional works of fine art are not sacrosanct canonical aesthetic objects to be differentiated from popular culture, but can be considered in more generalized studies as visual representations produced by people who disregard traditional distinctions between high and low art for deliberate reasons.[8] Studying the eighteenth-century illustrated imprints of Isaiah Thomas from this perspective, we find elements of both high and popular art, and we can move away from patronizing judgments based on traditional aesthetic theory and standards of pictorial representation, into a more nuanced understanding of the complicated history of visual culture.

These illustrated imprints may not exhibit a clear and abrupt change in printing practice, but they do give traces of a subtle, evolving movement in public taste, as addressed by Thomas, for the increased production of new, creative, and patriotic visual content in American reading matter. It is not so much a matter of whether he was an innovator or imitator in his use of illustrations; he was both. It is a more complicated story of change, with different turning points in different areas of production, and with a pace of change that accelerated over time. Frequently borrowed,

---

[8] Paul Jay, "Picture This: Literary Theory and the Study of Visual Culture," an address delivered at Convegno Internazionale sui Visual Studies, Rome, Italy, March 21, 2001. http://home.comcast.net/~jay.paul/jay.htm/.

occasionally original, the successfully marketed illustrated publications of Isaiah Thomas exemplify some of the traditional practices, subtle adaptations, and creative innovations taking place in cultural production in the early American republic.

Index

— Index —

www.ingramcontent.com/pod-product-compliance
Lightning Source LLC
Chambersburg PA
CBHW061756260326
41914CB00006B/1128